You Can Make Skittles

By Brian Birchall

To make skittles you will need

- Ten plastic bottles
- Half a bucket of sand
- Felt pens
- A funnel

Put some sand in each bottle.

Put the top back on each bottle.

Draw faces on the bottles
with the felt pens.

Now you have made skittles!

It is easy to play skittles.
Set up the skittles in rows.

One, two, three, four rows
of skittles.

Roll a ball at the skittles.

How many skittles can you knock over with one shot?

Put the skittles in rows again.

Count how many skittles you knock over.

You can play skittles by yourself
or with other people.

When you play skittles with other people,
you can keep score.

15

If you knock all the skittles over at once, it is called a **strike!**

16